Date: 6/2/15

J BIO HERSHEY
Ribke, Simone T.
Milton Hershey /

Milton Hershey

by Simone T. Ribke

Content Consultant

Nanci R. Vargus, Ed.D.
Professor Emeritus, University of Indianapolis

Reading Consultant

Jeanne M. Clidas, Ph.D.
Reading Specialist

Children's Press®
An Imprint of Scholastic Inc.
New York Toronto London Auckland Sydney
Mexico City New Delhi Hong Kong
Danbury, Connecticut

Library of Congress Cataloging-in-Publication Data

Ribke, Simone T.
  Milton Hershey / by Simone T. Ribke ; poem by Jodie Shepherd.
    pages cm. -- (Rookie biographies)
  Includes bibliographical references and index.
  Audience: Ages 3-6.
  ISBN 978-0-531-20594-5 (library binding : alk. paper) -- ISBN 978-0-531-20996-7
(pbk. : alk. paper) 1. Hershey, Milton Snavely, 1857-1945--Juvenile literature. 2. Hershey
Foods Corporation--Biography--Juvenile literature. 3. Businesspeople--United States--
Biography--Juvenile literature. 4. Chocolate industry--United States--History--Juvenile
literature. 5. Hershey (Pa.)--Juvenile literature. I. Shepherd, Jodie. II. Title.

  HD9200.U52H4758 2015
  338.7'664153092--dc23
  [B]

                              2014035678

Produced by Spooky Cheetah Press
Poem by Jodie Shepherd
Design by Keith Plechaty

© 2015 by Scholastic Inc.

Printed in China 62

SCHOLASTIC, CHILDREN'S PRESS, ROOKIE BIOGRAPHIES®, and associated logos
are trademarks and/or registered trademarks of Scholastic Inc.

1 2 3 4 5 6 7 8 9 10 R 24 23 22 21 20 19 18 17 16 15

Photographs ©: Alamy Images/Kristoffer Tripplaar: cover bottom; AP Images/The
Hershey Library via the Patriot-News: 12, 30 top right; Corbis Images/Bettmann:
cover top, 4, 11, 30 top left, 31 center bottom, 31 bottom; Getty Images/Tom Mihalek/
AFP: 24; Hershey Community Archives, Hershey, PA: 3 top right, 8, 15, 16, 18, 23, 28, 30
center top, 31 top; Courtesy of Hershey Entertainment & Resorts: 20; iStockphoto/
traveler1116: 3 top left; Jerry Anderson: 27; Shutterstock, Inc.: cover center
(dcwcreations), 3 bottom (Lissandra Melo).

Map by XNR Productions, Inc.

Table of Contents

Meet Milton Hershey

Milton Hershey was a great **entrepreneur**. He came from a poor family and ended up one of the richest people in the United States. Hershey started one of the world's most famous chocolate companies. He used his money to help others.

Hershey was born on September 13, 1857, in Derry Township, Pennsylvania. His family moved around a lot. Hershey attended six or seven different schools before he was 14. That year, he left school to work as an **apprentice** to a candy maker.

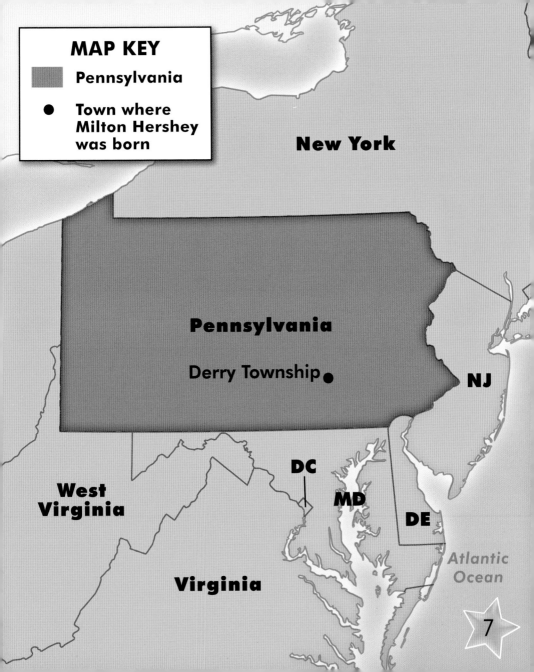

MAP KEY

Pennsylvania

● Town where Milton Hershey was born

New York

Pennsylvania

Derry Township ●

NJ

DC

West Virginia

MD

DE

Virginia

Atlantic Ocean

Hershey was not successful right away. But he worked very hard. He tried opening several businesses over the years. They all failed. In 1883, he started the Lancaster Caramel Company. This time, his business took off!

Hershey's mother, Fanny, taught him the importance of hard work. She always supported her son.

In 1893, Hershey went to the Columbian **Exposition** in Chicago, Illinois. A German company was showing how to make chocolate. At the time, it was a treat only for rich people. Hershey wanted to share it with everyone. But first he had to figure out a good recipe!

This is a scene from the Columbian Exposition.

Hershey began to experiment with making milk chocolate. In 1895, he started the Hershey Chocolate Company. The first chocolate items he sold were cocoa powder and chocolate-covered caramels.

In 1898, Hershey married Catherine "Kitty" Sweeney.

Sweet Success

In 1900, Hershey introduced the Hershey's bar. That same year, he sold his caramel company for an amazing $1 million. Hershey started building a new factory in Derry Church, Pennsylvania. Hershey chose Derry Church because it was close to dairy farms.

FAST FACT!

The Hershey's Kiss was first made in 1907.

14

This photo shows one of the earliest Hershey's bar wrappers.

The dairy farms supplied fresh milk for Hershey's chocolate. Derry Church is also close to the ports of New York and Philadelphia. That is where Hershey got the sugar and cocoa beans to make chocolate. The factory opened in 1905.

FAST FACT!

The Hershey Company uses between 300,000 and 350,000 gallons of fresh milk every day.

Hershey built a beautiful town near the factory. It had nice houses for the employees to live in. The town had schools, parks, and churches. Hershey built a trolley system for his workers to ride to and from work.

Kids play baseball on the field
Milton Hershey built for them.

In 1907, Hershey created Hersheypark as a place to have picnics. He later added a playground, a swimming pool, a zoo, and a bowling alley. There were also rides. Hersheypark became very popular and grew over time. Today, it is a large amusement park.

FAST FACT!

Hersheypark has more than 60 rides and 10 roller coasters.

Giving Back

Hershey and his wife were never able to have children. Together, they opened a school for orphan boys. They thought of these boys as their children. After Kitty died in 1915, her husband continued their **charitable** work.

FAST FACT!

Today, the Milton Hershey School also accepts girls. Each year, it serves about 1,900 children from struggling families.

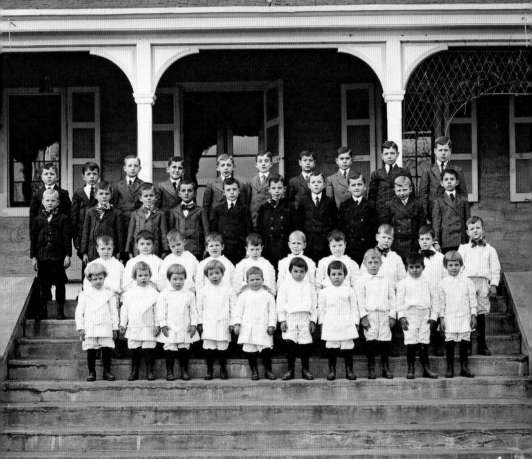

23

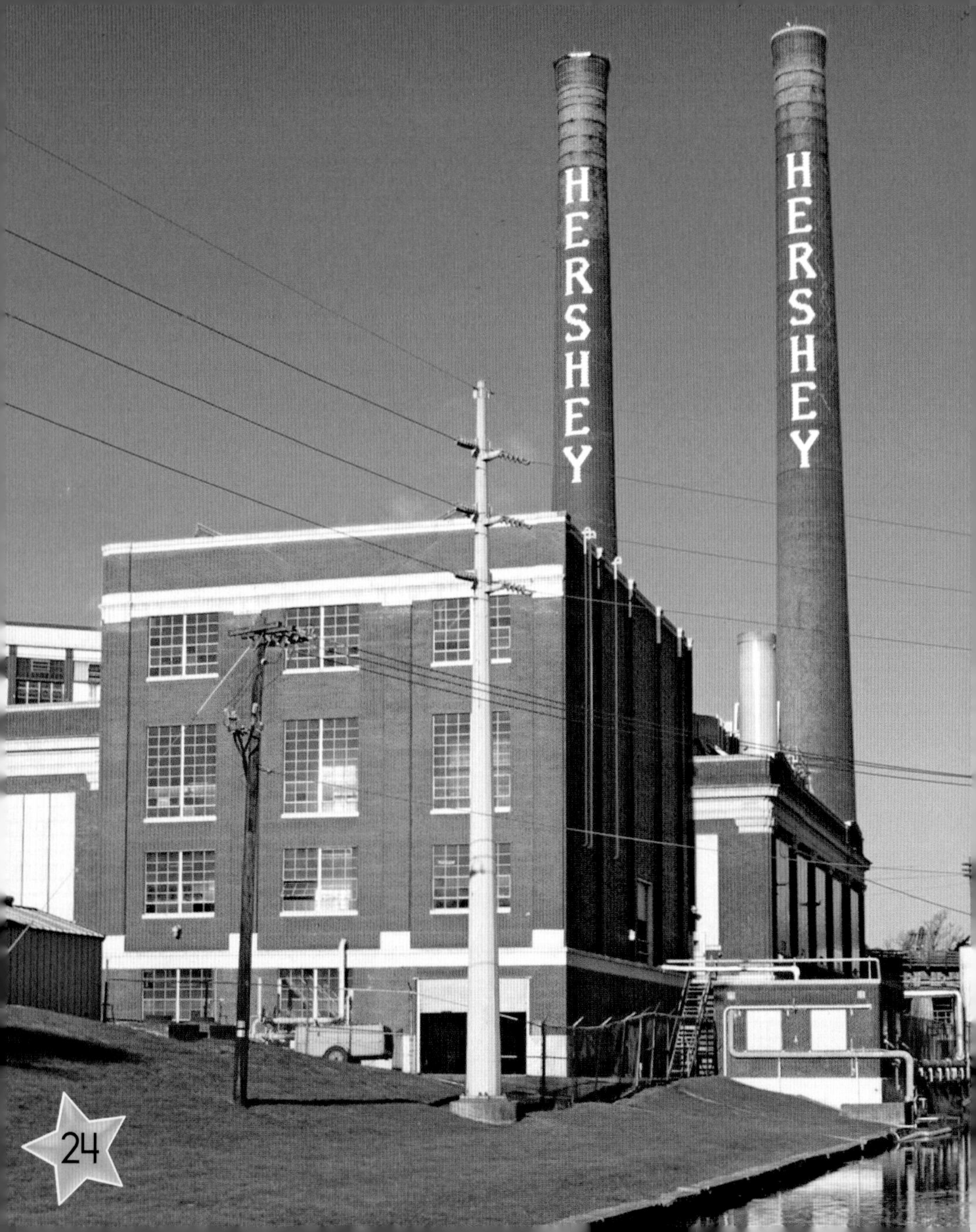
HERSHEY
HERSHEY

As Hershey grew older, his factory and town grew in size. So did his wealth. Hershey was very generous with his money. He gave most of it to the Hershey Trust Company. This company still uses his money to support the Milton Hershey School and other charities today.

Hershey was a hard worker. He continued to work until he was more than 80 years old. He died in Hershey, Pennsylvania, in 1945.

FAST FACT!

Hershey gave his home to the Hershey Country Club in 1930. He lived in a small upstairs apartment.

High Point Mansion was the Hersheys' home. It overlooked the chocolate factory.

Timeline of Milton Hershey's Life

1895
starts the Hershey Company

1857
born on September 13

1898
marries Catherine "Kitty" Sweeney

28

Milton Hershey worked hard to achieve his dreams. He never gave up, even when faced with failure. Hershey always gave help to his workers and others who had less than he did. His generosity continues to live on.

1900
sells his first Hershey's bar

1907
creates Hersheypark

1945
dies on October 13

A Poem About
Milton
Hershey

He brought milk chocolate to the USA

and gave a lot of his money away.

Next time you snack on a Hershey's Kiss,

about hardworking Milton, remember this:

help for those who need it; chocolate for those who eat it!

You Can Make a Difference

- Think about how you can help others in your community. Get involved.

- Never give up on yourself or your dreams, even if success does not come quickly.

Glossary

apprentice (uh-PREN-tiss): person who works for another in order to learn how to do a particular job

charitable (CHA-ruh-ta-buhl): person who gives money or other help to people in need

entrepreneur (on-truh-pruh-NOOR): person who starts a new business

exposition (eks-puh-ZISH-un): large public show that demonstrates how factories make things

Index

Facts for Now

Visit this Scholastic Web site for more information on Milton Hershey:
www.factsfornow.scholastic.com
Enter the keywords **Milton Hershey**

About the Author

Simone T. Ribke writes children's books and educational materials. She lives with her husband, children, and schnauzer in Maryland.